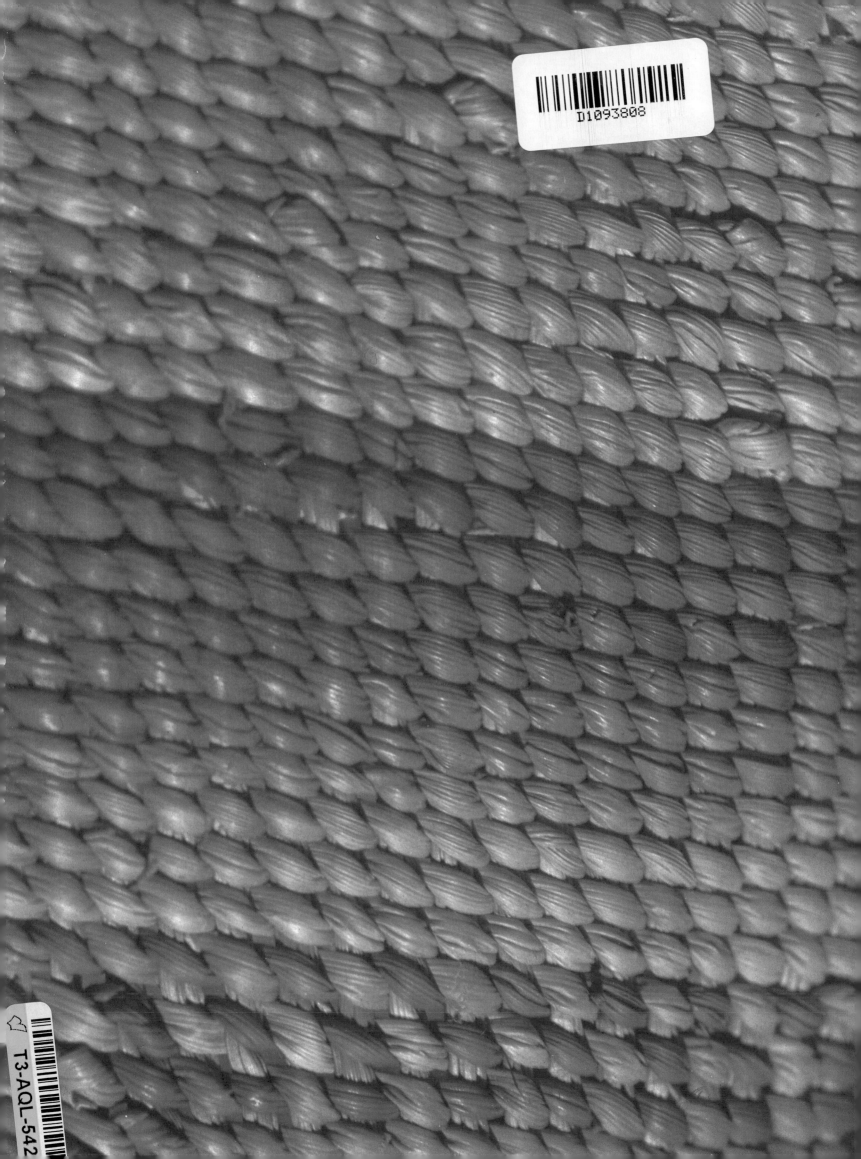

D1093808

T3-AQL-542

First published in 1984 by
Dorr/McLeod Publishing
20 Helen Street, West Heidelberg
Victoria, Australia 3081

© Neil McLeod (Photographer)
© Marji Hill (Text)

Designed by Mark Westaway – Neil McLeod
Typeset by Supertype
Printed in Hong Kong

**National Library of Australia
Cataloguing-in-Publication Data**

ISBN 0 949 433 06 3

This book is copyright. Apart from any fair dealing for the
purposes of private study, research, criticism or review
as permitted under the Copyright Act, no part may be
reproduced by any process without written permission
from the publishers.

ACKNOWLEDGEMENTS
Alex Barlow, Australian Institute of Aboriginal Studies, Canberra.
Dorothy Bennett, Arnhem Land Aboriginal Art Gallery, Darwin.
Jim Davidson, Oceanic and Aboriginal Art, Melbourne.
Steven Culley, Art/Craft Officer, Fremantle Prison, Western Australia.
National Museum of Victoria.
National Gallery of Victoria.
Robin Redlich, Photographer, Melbourne.
Malcolm Brownlee, Photographer, Melbourne.
Ralph Nicholls, Melbourne.
Tom Treasure, Ramingining, Northern Territory.
Tom Nell, U.S.A.
Mike Grant, Media, Churchlands College, Perth, Western Australia.
Peter Atkins, Melbourne.
David Gulpilil, Ramingining, Northern Territory.

**The publishers of this book express thanks to the
following contributors of photographs.**

J.V.S. Magaw, Flinders University, South Australia. Pages 55, 85/86.
Robert Edwards, International Cultural Corporation of Australia. Pages 27/28.
Jennifer Isaacs. Page 99.
Heidi Hebert. Page 98.
Geoff Lovell. Page 47/48.
National Museum of Victoria. Page 23.
Australian Information Service, Canberra. Pages 33, 35, 39/40, 104, 108, 111.
Nguiu Shire Council, Bathurst Island, Tom Nell. Pages 67/68.

Every effort has been made by the Publisher to
secure copyright clearance on all photographs
occurring in this book. Should any copyright
holder not have been contacted, or should there
be any copyright omission, then these people are
invited to come forward.

From the ochres of
MUNGO
Aboriginal Art Today

Marji Hill-Neil McLeod

DORR/McLEOD PUBLISHING

From the ochres of
MUNGO

Contents

Aboriginal Art is alive and well today

Aboriginal art springs from a heritage founded in great antiquity, and represents a continuity from the past to a tradition that today is certainly very much alive, dynamic, and a product of a complex and sophisticated culture.

In many parts of Australia, Aboriginal societies were devastated by European invaders and a great deal of their culture was subsequently destroyed. Today, however, many Aborigines are trying to piece together those preserved treasures of culture that have survived. In other areas of Australia conquest came later and its effect on Aboriginal culture has not been as severe as in the south eastern parts of the continent. Tradition based Aboriginal life-styles survive in parts of north Queensland, Northern Territory, South Australia and Western Australia, despite incredible pressures from contact with general Australian culture. Certainly traditional life-styles have been modified but the ideology or world view remains essentially the same. While many features of European life – goods and technologies, such as guns, trucks, clothing, food, alcohol, money, electronics – have been incorporated into Aboriginal culture, traditional beliefs and values are strong and in many areas there is a resurgence to revitalise them. The 'out-station' or 'homelands' movement is a particular expression of this. This movement involves small groups leaving the settlements and returning to live on their traditional lands.

The average white Australian often looks on Aboriginal art as being a relic of some past era. Even the culture itself is equated with the past, something that existed prior to European settlement. Many people fail to understand that Aboriginal culture is capable of change and innovation: some want to fossilise it, to prevent it from being contaminated by outside or alien influences. They don't want any part of that culture to change and especially not its art. They prefer it to be locked away in a time capsule. This look at Aboriginal art will show that it is not a product of a bygone era and that it is living and practised today. Not only have the traditional motivations for producing it persisted, but the art has adapted to changing circumstances and to external stimuli, just as it did prior to European contact. For centuries Macassan traders from what is now Indonesia sailed to the northern coasts to collect trepang, and the contact was recorded in the art of the region.

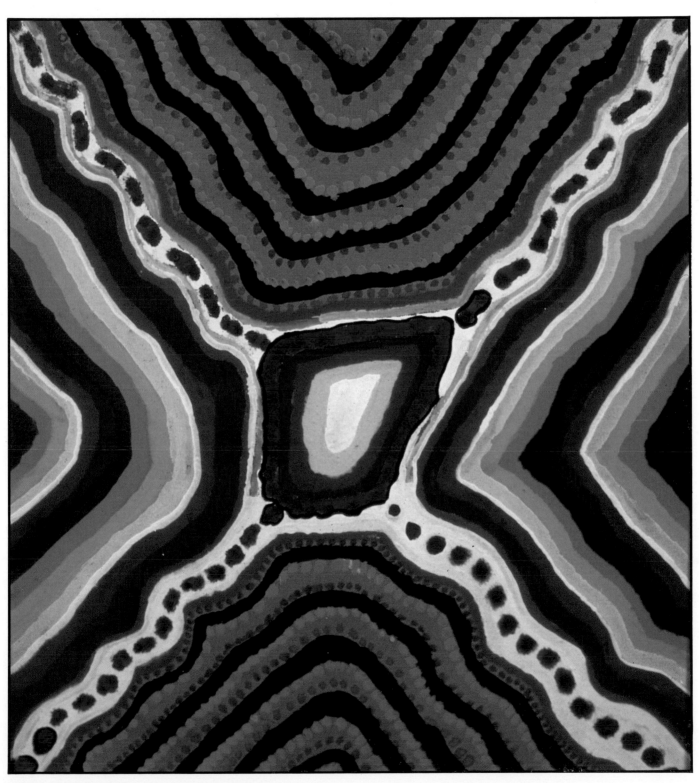

Percy Bulgardie – 'The Two Rainbows'.

Bark Painting – Groote Eylandt, Northern Territory.

Jimmy Pike – 'Rainbow Serpent Story'.

Jimmy Pike – 'Man Chained'.

Unfortunately art dealers and entrepreneurs, when considering Aboriginal art, have tended to regard objects as not being 'genuine' if produced outside the 'time capsule'. They had a vested interest in old art objects because of their investment potential. Anything not old were regarded as souvenirs, something especially made for the tourist market. Such attitudes have tended to downgrade contemporary Aboriginal art. It now seems that attitudes are changing slowly.

Certainly some Aboriginal art does fall into the category of souvenir, just as some art objects do in all other art traditions throughout the world. The problem with souvenirs, or art produced for the mass market, is that standards are lowered because such items, regardless of quality, are bought readily by an undiscerning public. Because Aboriginal art and culture is experiencing a revival much of the work now being produced represents a contemporary fine art tradition as genuine as that before European settlement. Not only is it still in some cases produced for religious reasons, but it is also providing Aboriginal groups with an economic base through the manufacture of works for sale to Europeans. These works often combine innovation with tradition to produce new, dynamic styles that should excite any art collector, for they are both beautiful and unique.

Most Aboriginal contemporary art is bought by foreign collectors and leaves Australia. Australians themselves have not as yet fully appreciated the fine art tradition that exists on their doorsteps. As one writer, Peter Cooke (1982:5) reflects:

Aboriginal art remains conspicuously absent from most of our public buildings and from offices of the new breed of fervently patriotic Australian companies. The glossy pages of the house and garden magazines attest the importance the wealthy place on owning fine art, yet Aboriginal art is again conspicuously absent from most of the nation's 'glorious homes'.

Aboriginal art is being appreciated in some art quarters, however. A few Aboriginal artists have shown their work in recent exhibitions in the capital cities; others have been invited to participate in major art events such as *Perspecta* and the *Biennale* in Sydney; and sponsorship is being given to touring exhibitions of Aboriginal art in Australia and overseas. The Aboriginal Arts Board of the Australia Council funds Aboriginal artists, for one of its major briefs is to promote the development of excellence in Aboriginal art.

Bobby Ngainmira, Gunwinggu group.

Percy Bulgardie.

Djugin – Ganalbingu group. Feathered djerrk.

misconceptions

For almost two centuries now, ever since Europeans first arrived on Australian shores and invaded Aboriginal lands, they have held negative views of Aboriginal cultures. Aborigines, they believed, lived an exceedingly 'primitive' life-style. Such attitudes are still to be found among average Australians. Most believe that Aboriginal culture is inappropriate to the modern world – that it is a palaeolithic survival, having only curiosity value. Aboriginal art in this type of thinking is simply a remnant of a dying culture. Such misconceptions and stereotypes need to be corrected. Consider how they came about.

In 1788 when the British first arrived, they already held preconceptions about Aborigines. Their ideas had been shaped by a unilineal theory of cultural development, later known as 'social Darwinism'. Very simply, the British believed that anyone living a hunter-gatherer life-style lived in a savage and primitive way. Societies were believed to evolve culturally past 'savagery' through 'barbarism' to finally reach 'civilisation'. The British with their superior, ethnocentric notions thought of themselves as the pinnacle of 'civilisation' while Aborigines were placed at the base of this scale of human cultural development. So Aborigines were seen as 'primitive', that is, being the first of a kind and living a very simple life-style.

The British arrived determined to take possession of the continent. Because explorers had not seen any evidence of agriculture, villages, buildings – the kinds of things they associated with 'civilisation' – they concluded that the land was not used and that there was no recognisable form of government. Under the prevailing ideas of international law the British felt free to claim the land as their own.

In fact, Aborigines did have a civilisation. The British should have explored further because, while there was no sign of a recognisable civilisation, there was evidence of a very sophisticated and highly complex culture. Aborigines used the land, were involved in land tenure, had a system of government and a complex system of social organisation based on religion and law. Not only this but Aborigines also had many different languages, had developed alternative communication systems and were masters of an effective technology.

Coming of White Man'.

Detail – 'Coming of White Man'.

Nineteenth century notions of social superiority which put European cultures at the apex and hunter-gatherers at the base are no longer acceptable. Such theories were refuted many years ago. People who still hold to them are behind the times. Notions of 'primitive' and 'savage' are in a sense a hangover from this dated theory of human cultural development. When one looks closely at Aboriginal art and culture it becomes quite clear that to describe it in terms of 'primitive' is misleading. On the contrary, Aboriginal art represents highly developed traditions which parallel those of the Western world. Furthermore, Aboriginal culture has proven to be very resilient; it is not dying out, and it is not the static, Stone Age culture that so many people have made it out to be.

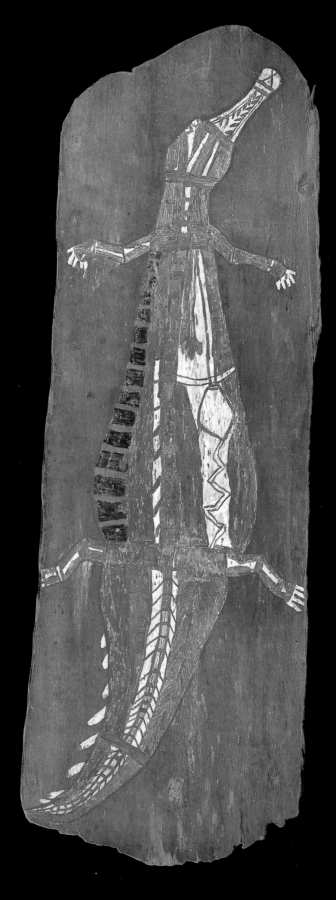

Early bark painting from the Baldwin Spencer Collection, National Museum of Victoria.

Djarrdi Ashley – Wagilag group,
Mulgurrum, North East Arnhem Land.

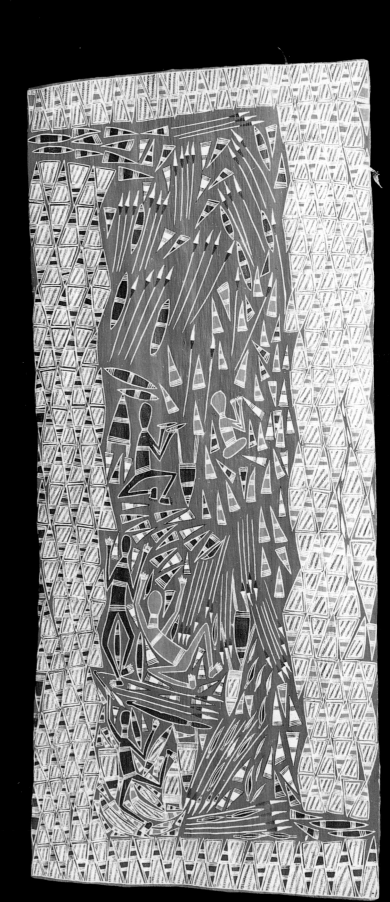

Antiquity

Despite its great antiquity, Aboriginal art continues to be relevant in the modern world, and should be of special interest to present day Australians.

The origin of Aboriginal man in this country dates back at least 40,000 years. This is the dating that most scientists agree on, although there are various claims that the genesis of Aboriginal man can be pushed back as far as 100,000 years or more. These older dates are essentially speculative. Many Aborigines, following their religious tradition, believe they originated in Australia and did not come from anywhere else. Prehistory is a very young discipline in this country, and excavated sites are relatively few, so that the dating of original occupation could very well be pushed back earlier than 40,000 years.

Art is part of this remote age. As far back as 30,000 years, evidence shows art was a concern of the Aborigines. The conscious use of pigment, particularly red ochre, for ritual purposes demonstrates this. Red ochre was found on the skeletal remains of a male corpse found at Lake Mungo in New South Wales. As the pigment was unavailable locally it must have been transported to the area in some quantity. Professor John Mulvaney (1981:22) believes personal adornment to be of great antiquity. Apart from the possible use of ochre for cosmetic and ritual purposes, other examples of body decoration have been discovered. At Kow Swamp in northern Victoria, a body around 12,000 years old was found with its head ornamented with a row of kangaroo incisors. Excavations at other sites have also found ancient efforts of personal adornment.

It is difficult to date rock paintings. One can only speculate that this form of art may have been done for thousands of years. Rock markings, however, are known to be very ancient. At Koonalda Cave on the Nullabor in South Australia, the wall markings are believed to be perhaps Australia's oldest example of art. They were made by drawing the fingers across the soft, chalky wall, or by abrading grooves on it and may be 20,000 years old. Excavations elsewhere have found other examples of rock art that date from prehistory.

While rock paintings are difficult to date, in Arnhem Land there are numerous paintings which could be several thousand years old, because in them are depicted two animals which have been extinct for around 3000 years. These are the Tasmanian tiger and the Tasmanian devil. Recent evidence suggests that some rock paintings may even date from the last Ice Age.

Pilbara, near Dampier, Western Australia.

Koonalda Cave, Nullabor Plain, South Australia

Lake Mungo, New South Wales.

Rock engraving of a Thylacine (Tasmanian Tiger) near Nourlangie Rock, Kakadu National Park, Northern Territory.

Pilbara, near Dampier, Western Australia.

Cultural context

An aesthetic response to any art form is heightened by an understanding of the cultural context in which it is produced and used. Aboriginal people today still paint sacred designs for ceremonial purposes; they still visit sacred sites, some of which may contain rock art; and, the traditional themes still persist. This would seem to suggest that the religious motivations for producing the art are still relevant. While Aborigines may have incorporated many material elements into their culture as a result of European contact, the Aboriginal world view – their religious ideology – has not disappeared. Essentially, the old values remain.

Major Differences Between Aboriginal Art and Western Art

The major difference between Aboriginal art and Western art is one of emphasis. Western art tends to be a reflection of the artist's personal vision of experience. As such it can be isolated out from the artist's culture and examined as a work of art by applying to it objective criteria of Western excellence and aesthetic appeal. Aboriginal art, generally speaking, does not represent that same personal vision – for the designs and motifs of Aboriginal art are culturally standardised, representing a collective vision of experience; they do not mean different things to different artists. Anthropologist Nicolas Peterson (1981:44) on this theme says:

> … in Aboriginal society the full impact of the art is available to all those who have reached the stage where they have been introduced to the inner realms of secret religious knowledge.

Another difference lies in the function of art. In Western societies, apart from producing art for personal reasons, art at the societal level is often valued for its investment potential. In Aboriginal society, traditionally speaking, art is not an economic concern but a religious concern. It is mainly produced for ceremonial purposes. In some cases, though, it is produced for exchange. Within the religious context, Aboriginal art is a means of claiming title to land since most Aboriginal art contains meanings about the relationships between people, land and Dreamtime Beings. Art is also a form of literacy since through it Aborigines are able to communicate information concerning their religious beliefs.

Victorian Arts Centre, Melbourne. ▶

William Dobell.

Ian Fairweather.

Fred Williams.

David Malangi –
Ramingining, Arnhem Land,
'Dollar Note Painting'.

Religion

Aboriginal art frequently manifests the Dreamtime. The Dreamtime is a complex, metaphysical concept which essentially subsumes not only the past but the present and the future. Dreamtime beliefs explain the universe as it appears to Aborigines. They provide for the people a system of laws and guidelines by which they can live. The beliefs have their origin in the ancestral past, that period long ago, when the Dreamtime Beings, in a series of founding dramas, emerged from the subterranean world, moved over a featureless earth, and, by their deeds, brought into being the whole Aboriginal cosmos. The places where these Dreamtime Beings emerged, the places they visited, and the places where they finally disappeared become the waterholes, rivers, rocks, hills and all the features of the environment. At the same time they placed in this environment all of life – human, animal, bird, fish and plant – forming one interconnected system of· relationships linking back to the Dreamtime Beings. Often these Beings were both man and animal at the same time or they could change from one to the other. The features of the landscape having been shaped, the Dreamtime Beings left human children, and they themselves disappeared underground or went into the sea. Before they disappeared they formulated the sets of rules for all living things to live by – the law.

The Dreamtime Beings, however, never really vacated the land. They remain in it, though hidden, a vital force still, always retaining the power to intervene in the lives of men and women.

The power of the Dreamtime Beings is very important for Aborigines. Aborigines need access to this power because it helps boys become men and girls become women, helps increase the abundance of food, ensures fertility, and assists the spirits of the dead on their way to their resting places. The Dreamtime Beings, in return for helping the people, expect that they in turn will perform rituals, care for sacred sites, and generally care for each other. Thus there is a reciprocal and abiding relationship between people and the Dreamtime Beings.

Tom Djunpurrdurr, Jinbar group, Ramingining Arnhem Land. ▶

Dreamtime Beings remain hidden in the land, a vital force still, with the power to intervene in the lives of men and women.

Katajuta, mountains of many heads.

Bobby Bunungurr – Ganalbingu group.
'Water Lily Dreaming'.

The water lily features in many of **Bobby Bunungurr's** paintings because of its special Dreaming significance.

The performance of rituals is, therefore, very important. Key elements include the story-line, that is, the 'myth' pertaining to the deeds of a particular Dreamtime Being, songs, designs on art objects, dance, ritual paraphernalia and the special site associated with the ritual. In other words, Aborigines re-enact the events of the Dreamtime, integrating all the various forms of artistic expression in the ritual, and reactivating the spiritual force of those events.

Aboriginal art is usually made in the context of religious ritual. The actual making of the art objects puts their creators into contact with the Dreamtime Beings, enabling them to tap the ancestral power. The designs on the art objects are regarded as actual manifestations of the Beings. The artist in the process of creating reactivates the spiritual powers and brings them into a direct relationship with him enabling the power to be tapped. But to be able to achieve this, Aboriginal artists can only ever paint or carve those designs which are relevant to him or her in a spiritual sense. This does not mean the artist can just make anything of Dreamtime significance. There has to be that special totemic connection between artist, Dreamtime Being and the object being made. R. M. and C. H. Berndt with Stanton (1982:24) when describing this connection and relationship say it implies that the artist is

> a living representative of that being, a potential custodian of the rites and myths and songs associated with it.

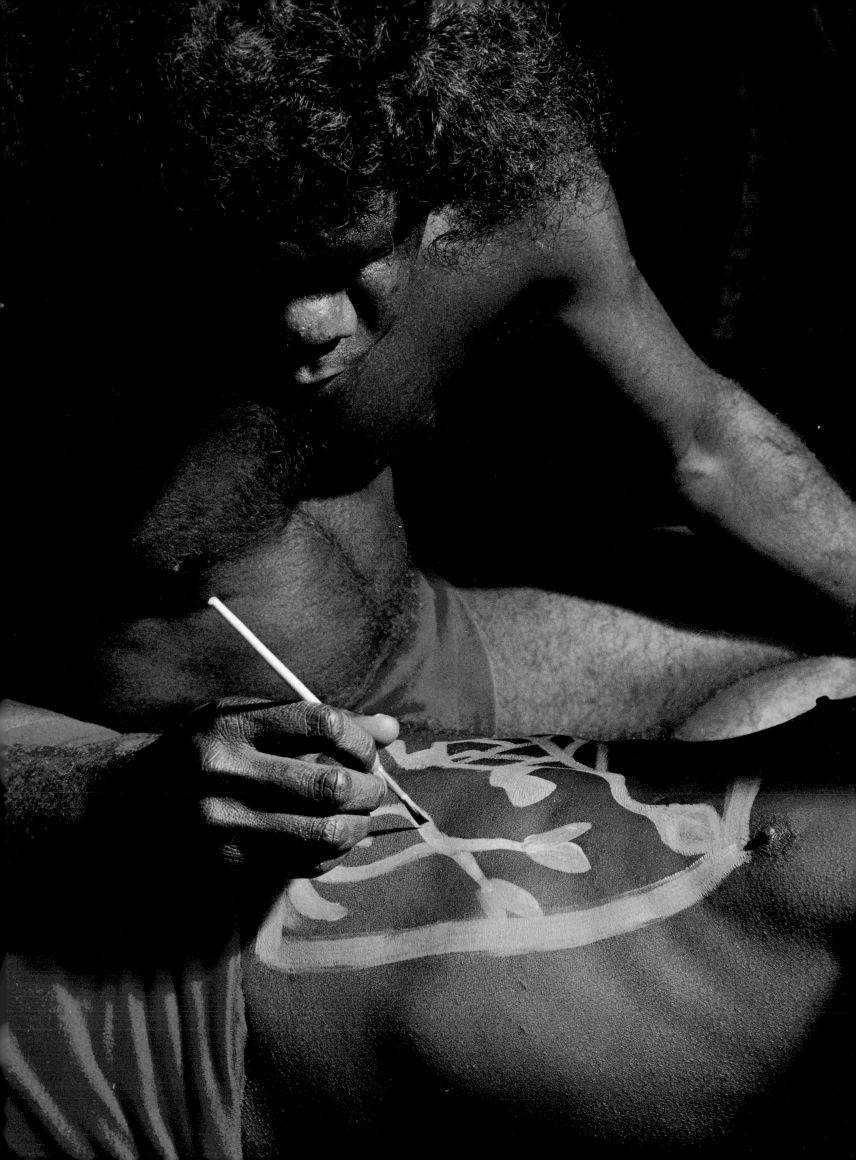

Mornington Island Dancers performing at the Victorian Arts Centre, Melbourne.

47

Stone arrangement on Ningham Station, Lake Moore outside Paynes Find, Western Australia.

Ownership

Designs and images on art objects, stories, songs, dances – all of these kinds of artistic expression are owned in Aboriginal society. Usually, the people belonging to or owning a certain stretch of territory are the only ones allowed to tell the stories associated with their 'country' or to depict these stories in any artistic medium or ritual. Generally speaking, other groups of people belonging elsewhere could not perform these rituals or tell the stories unless permission or collaboration had been sought from the owners. The system of ownership or the distribution of rights in such things varies throughout Australia.

Howard Morphy (1981:57) who has written extensively about art in north east Arnhem Land says that rights in art in northern Australia are vested in patrilineal clans or sections of those clans. But a person may have rights in the designs of his mother's clan and mother's mother's clan as well. This does not mean that just anyone from a clan can make a clan design; only those members with authority can do so – this is usually vested in the hands of senior male members. The senior male members of a clan decide when to teach younger members to make a design and when to explain the deep meanings of it. Only they have the authority to pass on information about their art's meaning to outsiders.

Arnhem Land. This is one of the most important stories of the Mararba Group, and shows the theme of snakes and fishtrap.

The fishtrap is made of large logs placed across a stream, and are depicted as horizontal bars. Between these bars are curved shapes representing mud holes filled with charcoal and seaweed. Barramundi fish are shown caught in the trap.

Mikaran the sacred snake of the Dreamtime, causes rain, thunder and lightning. His forked tongue pierces stormclouds (wavy lines) which have been formed by the breath of the snake (dots), and with the piercing of the clouds lightning runs across the sky and rain descends.

The sacred waterhole of Mikaran and his mate are shown in the centre of the painting. If a menstruating woman goes near this waterhole the snake smells her blood, just as the rainbow serpent smelt the blood of the Wawilak sisters in the Dreamtime. The woman must run away quickly, otherwise the snake will run after her and kill her. Even if she escapes, the snake will send lightning across the sky to chase her.

Ironwood carving, Melville Island, Northern Territory. ▶

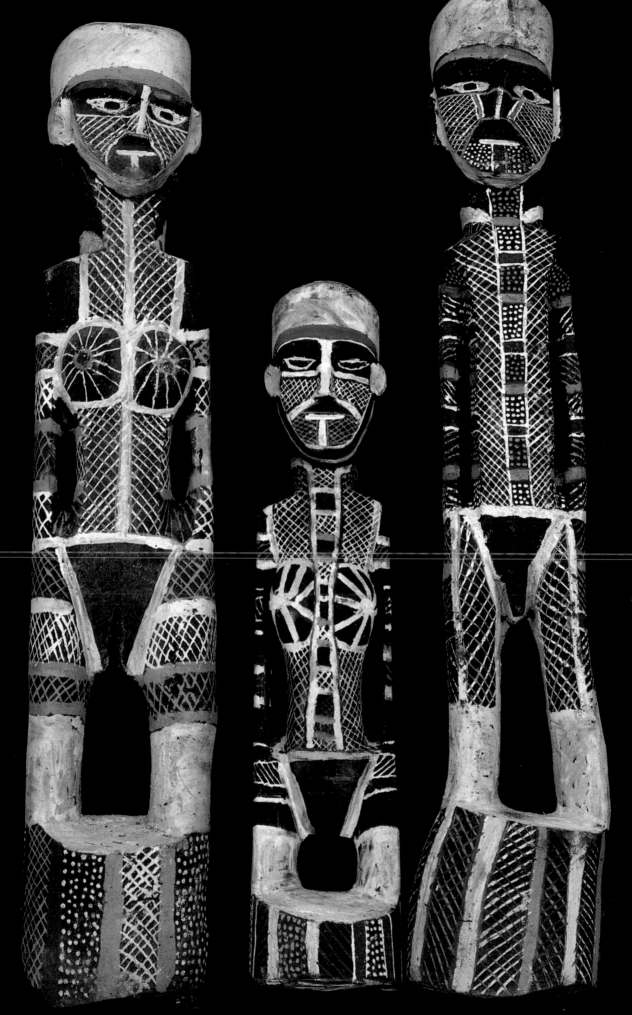

Art, Land and Dreamtime Beings

While Aborigines, like many other indigenous peoples, had no written language they did have a system to communicate ideas – a kind of visual literacy. Aboriginal art communicates beliefs. Essentially it relates people to their 'country' and also links both people and land to the Dreamtime.

It has already been said that the image or design on an art object is a manifestation of a Dreamtime Being or an event associated with that Being. A barramundi painted on a rock shelter may be the Barramundi Being; a kangaroo – the Kangaroo Being, and so on. The geometric, abstract elements of a bark painting may be the attributes of some particular Being while the 'U' shape around a set of concentric circles of a desert painting may tell of a Water Spirit Dreaming.

Not only does the art refer to the characters of the Dreamtime but it actually provides a connection between human beings and these superhuman powers to particular places in the landscape. The Dreamtime Beings that feature in art work are associated with specific parts of the country. Another way of looking at some Aboriginal art is to regard it as being like a map of the countryside for all the parts of the relevant landscape are to be found in the designs.

Because the designs and images made are owned by groups of people, art can also be said to link human beings to certain Dreamtime Beings. Howard Morphy (1981:62) in discussing the art of north eastern Arnhem Land says that each clan has a set of designs which are unique to it, and simply by looking at this design you can identify the clan to which it belongs. The design also tells you which Dreamtime Being is associated with that clan.

This is what Aboriginal art means to Aboriginal people. The complexity and sophistication of thought that goes into making it is such that it is totally misleading and an injustice to describe it as 'primitive' art.

Making an acrylic painting in the Desert style.

Fred Djdjbaka – 'Ngalyod the Rainbow Serpent', Oenpelli, Western Arnhem Land. 56

Ancestral woodcarving, North East Arnhem Land. ▲

Ancestral ironwood carving, Melville Isla

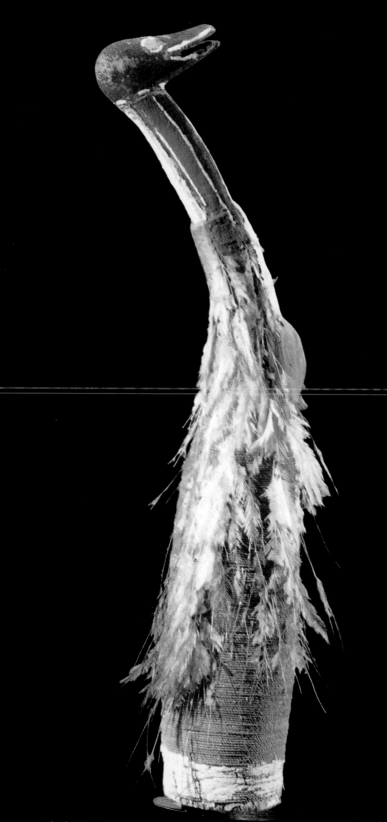

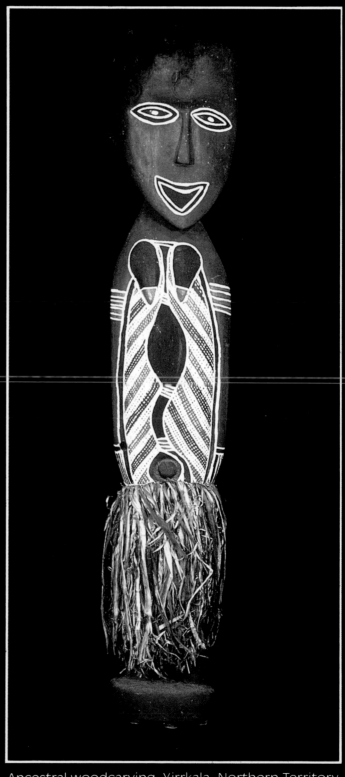

Ancestral woodcarving, Yirrkala, Northern Territory.

Birdcarving decorated with paperbark, string and ochres from Yirrkala, Northern Territory.

Woven dilly bags and baskets made by women from Arnhem Land

Forms and Styles

There is great variety of form and style in Aboriginal art, and styles tend to relate to different regions.

Forms of art include rock paintings and engravings, sculpture and wood carving traditions, sand sculptures, body painting, ground paintings, paintings on bark and on carvings, designs incised on ironwood, utilitarian objects, musical instruments and various other assemblages and objects. Apart from paintings and sculptures or three-dimensional forms that comprise an 'art' tradition in a formal sense, there is a wide ranging array of objects, either utilitarian or ceremonial, which constitute more a 'craft' tradition. Such items include dilly bags, baskets, mats, belts, arm bands, other ornaments and ritual paraphernalia. These items are made from feathers, plumes, furs, string, plant fibres, ochres, clay and anything else that can be gathered from the natural environment.

All of these individual forms traditionally would be found in some kind of ceremonial context – and would be integrated into the ritual performance. Because art objects were created for a particular ceremony they were not normally meant to be kept. Much of Aboriginal art is ephemeral. Sand sculptures, for instance, will be destroyed; a painting on a person's body may last for a few days only; the bark baskets used by the Tiwi to cover up a *pukamani* pole are deliberately destroyed or left lying on the ceremonial ground; and ground paintings are erased at the end of a ceremony. Even some things that are constructed of wood and which have the potential to last for a long time, such as the Tiwi *pukamani* poles are intentionally left to decay at the end of a ceremony; in time they will be eaten by white ants or they will disintegrate from exposure.

Ada Tipingwiti of Bathurst Island, Northern Territory, prepares a basket to be placed upside down over a tall *pukamani* pole in a Tiwi mortuary ceremony. ▶

▲ Making a *pukamani* pole, Bathurst Island, Northern Territory.

◀ *Pukamani* poles from completed mortuary ceremonies.

Decorated ceremonial spears from Melville Island, Northern Territory. ▶

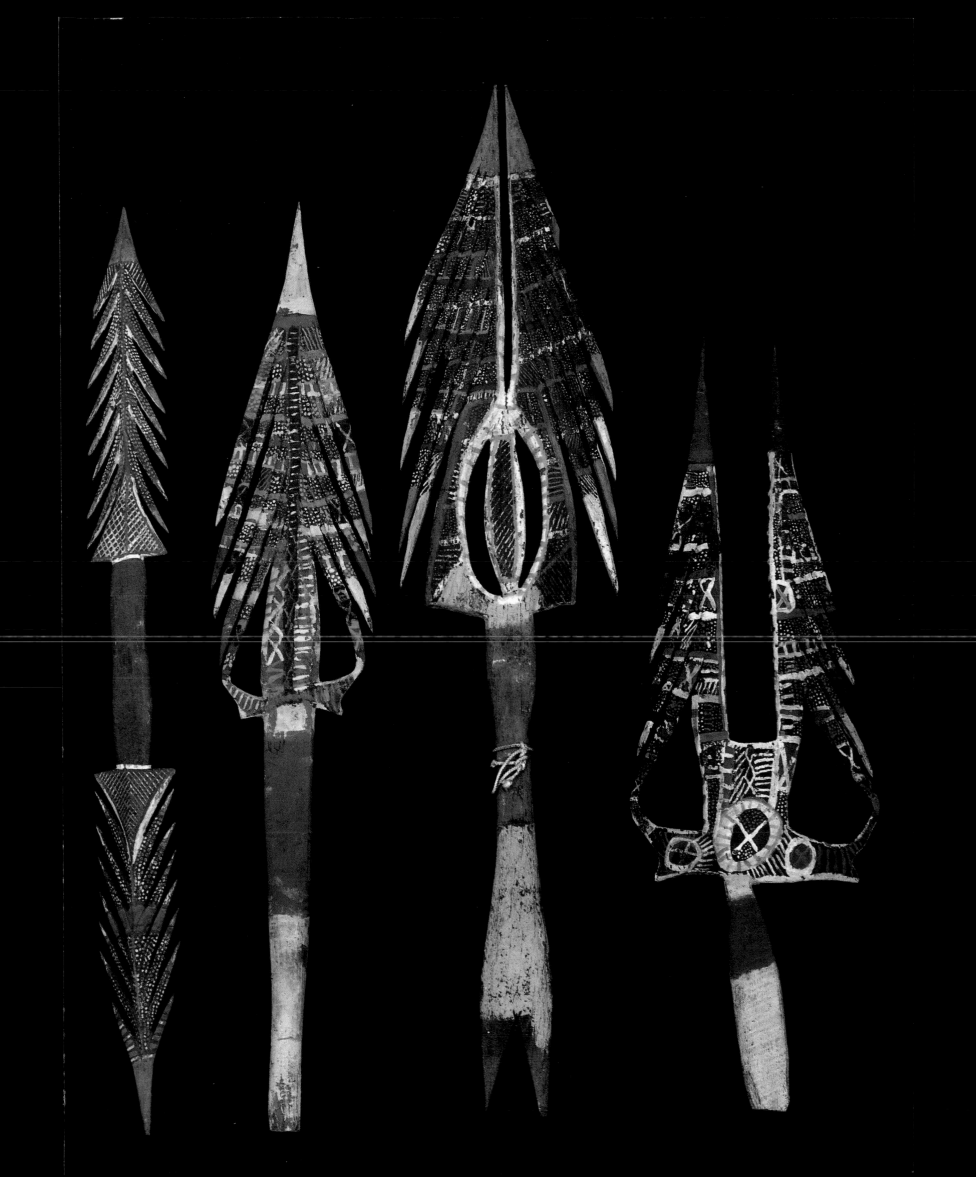

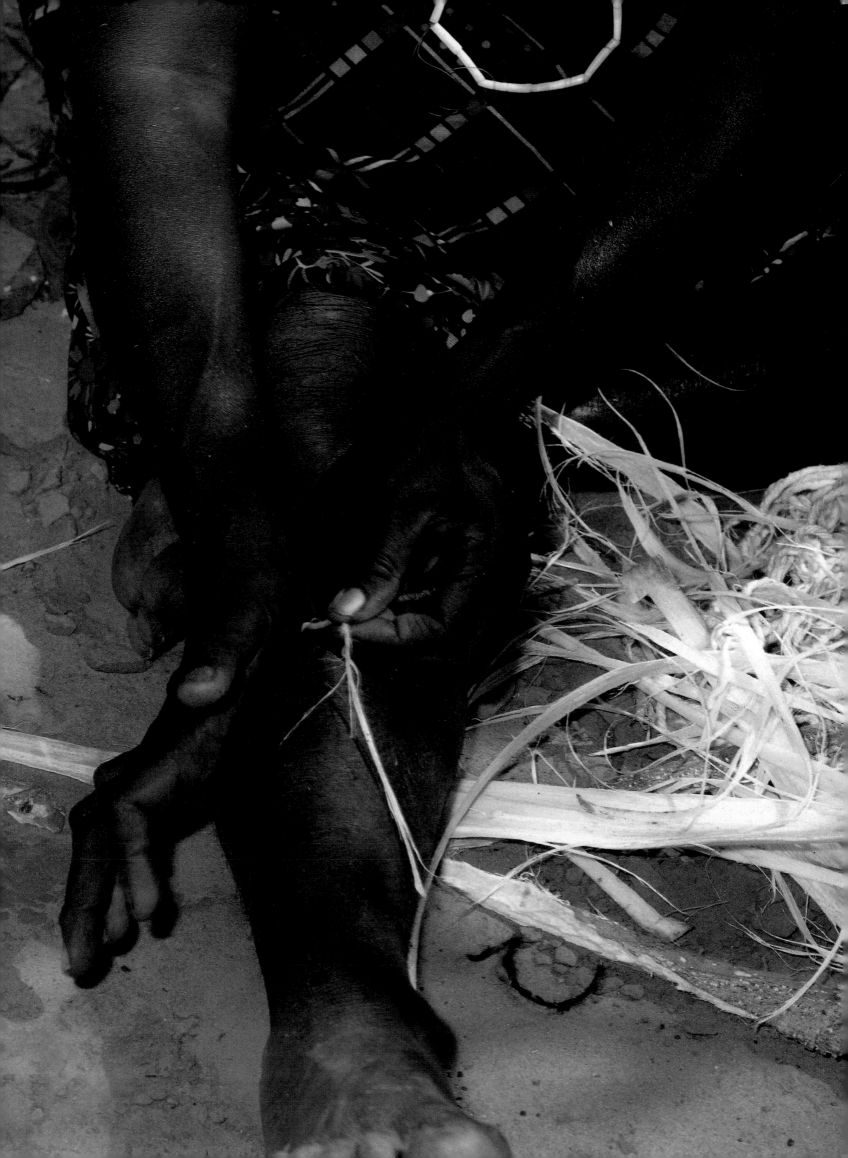

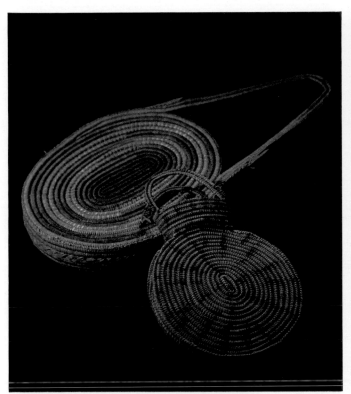

▲ Coiled baskets.

Reed basket made by **Thelma Carter.** ▲

◄ **Thelma Carter,** Lake Tyers, Victoria.

◄ Platting strands of bush string.

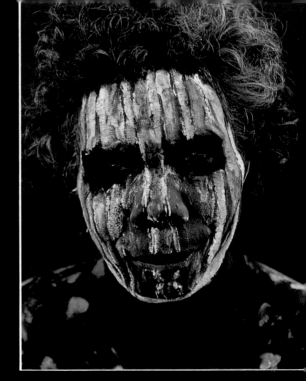

Painted faces and bodies, some featuring *pukamani* beards and headdresses

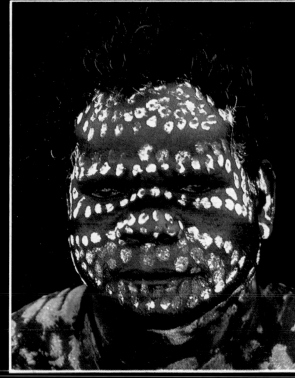

made of cockatoo feathers, Bathurst Island, Northern Territory.

Incised baobab nut, the Kimberleys, WA. In recent years these baobab nuts have become well known because of their appeal to tourists. Recent forms of this art work are more elaborate than the earlier, traditional examples which tended to depict geometric and figurative images.

Makinti – batik, Ernabella, Central Australia. ▶

Rock Paintings

In parts of Australia there are rock art galleries which present some of the most outstanding examples of rock art in the world. These open air galleries are located mainly in the Kimberleys (Western Australia), Arnhem Land (Northern Territory) and Cape York (Queensland), although there are plenty of other examples to be found elsewhere in Australia.

The Kimberley rock paintings offer an excellent example of the changes that have taken place in form, style and technique. While the Wandjina paintings there are well known, they represent a later development. The Wandjina tradition replaced an earlier one which consisted of the Bradshaw figures – small, graceful figures often depicted as dancing or running.

The Wandjina paintings are strange and mysterious. In the Dreamtime the Wandjinas travelled over the land and when they disappeared into it, they left their images on the rock walls. These images are characterised by huge man-like shapes sometimes in proportions more than seven metres tall. These spectacular images are partly human in form and partly cloud-like, manifesting the ambiguity of these Beings, which could exist either in human or cloud form. They are said to control clouds.

The Wandjina Beings are believed to be very powerful and must therefore be treated with great respect. Aborigines have to observe certain formalities on approaching their sites. They must call out to them, for instance, to inform them that a group of people is approaching. Their powers are both destructive and procreative. They control the distribution of Spirit children; but they may also avenge any disrespect by bringing monsoons, storms and floods. Offenders could be struck with lightning, or be drowned in floods. The monsoonal rains which sweep the area each year from December to March are believed to be the work of the Wandjinas, so it is very important for Aborigines to perform rituals to ensure that these powerful Beings are placated at all times.

Further artistic traditions on rock walls are found in the escarpment area of western Arnhem Land. Two broad stylistic traditions are evident. First, there is the *Mimi* style believed to represent the oldest tradition. *Mimi* art is characterised by the slender, stick-like figures which are usually depicted in one of the red ochre shades. *Mimi* figures are usually depicted in action poses – running, hunting, throwing weapons and dancing. Aborigines believe these paintings to be the work of the benevolent but timid *Mimi* spirits which inhabit the caves and clefts of rocks in the escarpment.

71

Wandjina art site, Gibb River Station, Western Australia.

The other style, X-ray art, is considered to be more recent than *Mimi* art. Paintings of animals, birds, reptiles, fish and human beings executed with various colours, characterise it. The image is usually shown against the plain background of the rock wall. Not only is the external shape of the subject matter depicted but the internal structures – backbone, lungs, heart, kidneys and other organs – are painted as well. In contrast to the action poses of *Mimi* art, X-ray paintings are generally static and sometimes of imposing proportions. The X-ray style is also used on bark paintings.

Western Arnhem Land rock paintings also indicate change or innovation. Sometimes the images reflect the contact that has been made between Aborigines and peoples of other lands. There are many images of Macassan prows, European sailing ships, guns, and so on. One rock shelter, according to Elaine Godden (1982:38) even has images of a ship, a cowboy with wide hat and clothing, a cat, and the Sydney Harbour Bridge! There is evidence that Aboriginal artists were painting on rocks in this area as recently as the 1960s. While very few rock paintings are the work of present day artists, the stories and subject matter of the rock art are still known to a number of people. They are very important for the recording of this tradition of rock painting and of its meaning.

Many painted rock galleries were rediscovered in the country surrounding Laura, a small township in Cape York. These galleries, the Quinkin galleries, like their counterparts in Arnhem Land and the Kimberleys, reflect different art traditions. Paintings are frequently superimposed one over the other, sometimes as many as ten layers. Not only are there images reflecting the traditional religious motifs, hands, feet, weapons, animals, reptiles, birds and humans, but these images also show something of the contact with Europeans of the area. There are horses carrying men with guns, and there are men wearing clothing such as hats, boots and shirts.

Given the various artistic traditions found even within rock painting and given the fact that rock painting has been a form practised right into this century it is hardly appropriate to describe rock painting as 'paleolithic' or 'Stone Age' art. The complexity of style and the sophistication of form and image parallel that to be found in all Aboriginal painting forms.

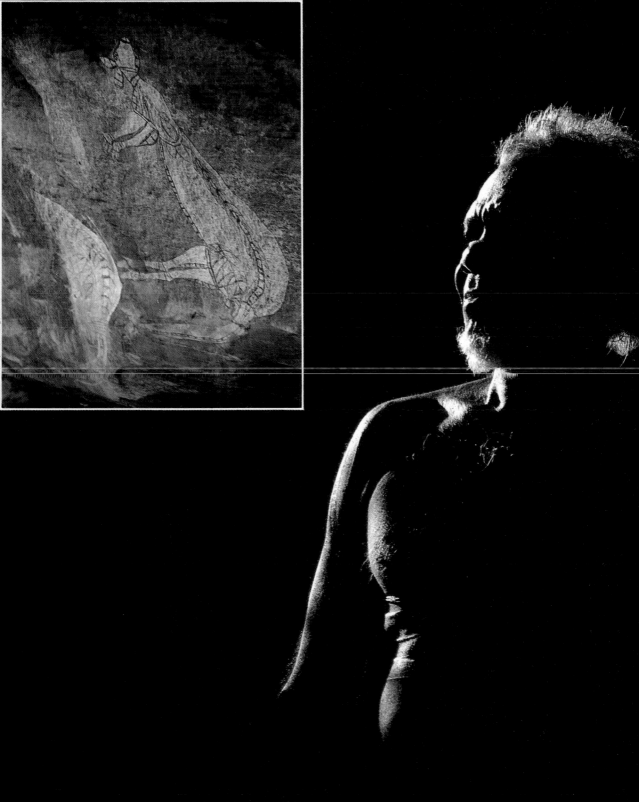

X-Ray Art and the artist, **Bobby Ngainmira**

▲ *Quinkin* rock paintings, Cape York, Queensland.
◄ Kakadu National Park, Northern Territory.
Inset, *Mimi* figures on rock surface, Kakadu.

Bark Painting

Bark painting is a tradition found in northern Australia, particularly in Arnhem Land, although it has been reported in other areas of Australia as well. There are distinct stylistic differences within this form, the two commonly known ones being the western Arnhem Land figurative style and the geometric, abstract style usually found in north east Arnhem Land. While these styles are distinctive of these parts of Arnhem Land, they are not necessarily exclusive to the areas. Figurative paintings can be found in eastern Arnhem Land while the geometric styles can also be found in the western parts.

The figurative style, the X-ray images of animals, birds, reptiles, and humans, that are found painted in rock shelters in the escarpment area, is also painted on bark, either by itself or in relation to other figures. In these figurative bark paintings the image, with all the internal and external details, is painted on to a plain, ochred background.

In contrast to paintings of western Arnhem Land those of the east break the whole surface of the bark up into compartments. There is a base colour, a border, dividing lines and figurative or geometric images. These images are symbolic representations of different aspects of a Dreamtime story. Each element of the painting may mean a variety of things in different contexts. Howard Morphy (1981:61) explains a painting about the Wild Honey Ancestor of eastern Arnhem Land. He identifies all the geometric patterning and shows how each element is a part of the story, for example, the diamonds are the cells of the hive; the cross-hatching infill is the different components of the hive – the grubs, the honey and the bees – while the other geometric components represent further details associated with wild honey.

There are many levels of meaning in these bark paintings. One may be the public meaning – a version that can be communicated to anyone, including Europeans who may buy one of the paintings. Then there are the deeper layers of meaning which can only be told over time to properly initiated male members of the clan.

Bobby Ngainmira –
Gunwinggu group, Oenpelli, Arnhem Land.

George Milpurru –
Mulgurrum, North East Arnhem Land.

Previous pages,
Removing the bark from the tree,
Burning removes excess fibre and flattens the
bark.

Ground Paintings

Ground paintings are a form found in the desert regions of Central Australia. For a long time art of the desert remained unknown to non-Aborigines. This was probably due to its secret-sacred nature being the property of religious cults and initiated men, and to its ephemeral nature. At the end of religious rituals the ground paintings were destroyed, and other art works, for example religious paraphernalia, designs on shields or bodies, were dismantled or wiped out.

Ground paintings were produced only in parts of the desert. The artists spread broken-up termite mound on a selected area of ground, softened it with water into a thick paste and patted the surface to a required shape. Once the surface was prepared the designs were laid on it with coloured ochres and feather down. Ground paintings are manifestations of certain totemic sites, especially those associated with the emergence and disappearance of important Dreamtime Beings. In those areas where ground paintings were not made, the same designs are painted onto shields to be used in religious rituals. Ground paintings were always made to the accompaniment of singing.

Desert art is characterised by abstract, geometric and schematic elements. The images consist of spirals, lines, circles and points combining around 14 basic graphic elements. To Aboriginal people of the desert regions these graphic elements are said to represent the hunter's eye view of the world. Nicolas Peterson (1981:47), one of a very few anthropologists who have written about desert art, says that the motifs derive from the marks left on the ground by humans, animals and objects: it is as if these marks are seen from above. The marks over time have been stereotyped and simplified into an artistic system consisting of the basic graphic elements. As with the art of eastern Arnhem Land it has many layers of meaning and the designs, together with their various combinations, can be open to differing interpretations. Only those fully initiated into the culture would ever know the total, sacred meanings.

Artists-in-residence at Flinders University, South Australia, making paintings in the Desert style.

Detail of a Papunya painting, Central Australia.

Early in the 1970s an innovation in painting made desert art better known. An art teacher, Geoffrey Bardon, encouraged the traditional artists to paint their designs on hardboard and canvas and to use Western acrylic paints and brushes. The Papunya Tula artists group, which developed this style, began producing highly acclaimed and exciting works of art in a Western medium but at the same time still using the traditional desert designs. Despite the innovations in medium, technique and colours, the Papunya paintings reflect the distinctive desert style, and are now eagerly sought after by fine art collectors both in Australia and overseas.

Sculpture and Wood Carving

Sculpture in Aboriginal Australia usually takes the form of three-dimensional wood-carving. Wood-carving traditions are diverse and, as with the painting traditions, forms and style differ regionally. Often wood carvings are combined with painting, for it is not unusual to find painted designs on wood-carvings, such as mortuary posts.

Wood carvings are a characteristic art form right across northern Australia. Apart from the renowned carved posts of Arnhem Land and some of its off-shore islands, there are small wood carvings – numerous and varied – such as message sticks, carved totemic animals and Macassan type pipes. Artists in north east Arnhem Land make carved figures in human and quasi-human form, usually depicting Dreamtime Beings. They also make *rangga*, secret-sacred poles and *wurumu*, mortuary posts. As part of mortuary ceremonies they make hollow-log coffins, into which the bones of a dead person are placed after careful ritual preparation. The coffin is then stood upright in the ceremonial ground.

Bathurst and Melville Islands, the home of the Tiwi, have *pukamani* poles elaborately carved and painted with clan designs. They resemble the Arnhem Land posts, and like them are used in mortuary ceremonies. *Pukamani* ceremonies are designed to settle and control the spirit of the dead person, preventing it from causing trouble and misfortune in the land of the living.

Stella Munkara – making an ironwood figure, Bathurst Island, Northern Territory. ▶

Gulpilil playing the didjeridu. ▶

◀ Decorated wooden carrying vessel, Western Desert.

The west coast of Cape York Peninsula has a distinctive wood-carving tradition. Carved figures — both human and animal — are used in Wik-mungkan rituals. They are totemic carvings to be used at special sites, where dances are performed which re-enact Dreamtime events.

Wood-carving traditions are also found in the desert areas and in south eastern regions of Australia. Carved shields, weapons, utensils and sacred boards represent the tradition in the desert.

The wood-carving tradition of south east Australia deserves particular attention. Art of this area has never received much prominence and until recently was quite unknown. This is because of the cultural devastation that took place in areas such as south Queensland, New South Wales, Victoria and parts of South Australia. Aborigines living traditional life-styles disappeared and knowledge of their art disappeared with them. In recent years, however, Aborigines have been trying to piece together some of this almost lost culture.

Carol Cooper (1981:29) says that the distinctive features of the art of this region are:

> The style of line and mysterious intent of (the) designs, sculpted from the living wood of standing trees, or finely carved with often chiaroscuro effect.

The wood-carving tradition that she discusses includes carved weapons (shields, clubs, boomerangs, spear throwers) and carved trees. Other art forms of this region include decorated skin cloaks, body painting, stone arrangements, stone sculpture and rock art. The designs found on wood or other objects here are believed to represent the country of its creators. They also are concerned with displaying personal and group identity and the relationship of people to their lands. In this the designs follow those used in other art forms from other regions.

Making a boomerang. ▶

Innovation

Apart from Aboriginal art being of interest to tourists or to entrepreneurs out to collect 'genuine' items for investment, Aboriginal art has been evolving a contemporary Australian tradition in its own right. Alongside non-Aboriginal art that of the Aborigines is moving into the realm of art for its own sake, and in some cases is even providing Aboriginal groups with a livelihood through the sale of their works as fine art. While Aboriginal art is still made for traditional religious reasons the motivation to make art for economic purposes runs parallel.

Many people are of the opinion that Aboriginal art should not be dissociated from its culture, for to do so may mean misunderstanding what Aboriginal art signifies for Aboriginal people. There is an alternative view which holds that it is possible to view Aboriginal art simply as art, that it does have universal, aesthetic appeal according to general art criteria. Both standpoints are equally tenable and both perspectives should be considered in any analysis of Aboriginal art. Simply to see *only* what it means from the perspective of its creators is to undervalue its beauty and appeal.

In recent years Aboriginal art has experienced change and innovation partly as a response to external stimuli and partly because it has always (even before European contact) been prepared to incorporate change. Innovations took place in Aboriginal art long before Europeans arrived, an excellent example being that of the Macassan influence on Aboriginal culture in Arnhem Land. Macassans had been coming each year to the northern shores of Australia for centuries and the effects of this contact can be found in the images of much of the art. Innovations demonstrate the readiness of a culture to adapt to other influences to maintain a healthy, dynamic tradition.

Making a clay pot, Bathurst Island, Northern Territory. ▶

Neville Gable and

Reg Moolarvie – painting in the European illustrative tradition, Western Australia.

Wendy Feifer-Nannup – Aboriginal painting in the European illustrative tradition. She has had several exhibitions and is planning a show in London.

Innovations in Aboriginal art have built on already existing foundations. Aboriginal artists have explored different ways of treating traditional subject matter and in many cases they have incorporated new themes. They have also looked at different media and techniques to develop their traditional themes.

Innovations occur in various regions. In north east Arnhem Land, as with western Arnhem Land, innovative styles have developed within the limits of the traditional themes. So while the subject matter has remained constant different ways of depicting the traditional ideas have been investigated.

In 1982 an exhibition of 'Aboriginal art at the Top' presented by the Museums and Art Galleries of the Northern Territory gave excellent examples of contemporary, innovative Aboriginal art. One hundred and five artists were represented which gave some idea of the breadth of Aboriginal visual art and the range of objects produced for sale. The exhibition pointed to the fact that traditional art was still being produced in a contemporary context and yet there were developments indicative of a dynamic and exciting tendency in Aboriginal culture.

It is impossible to talk about innovations and not mention the work of the Papunya Tula artists' group from Central Australia. Coming from the desert are perhaps some of the most exciting masterpieces much sought after by the art market. Traditional designs which used to be put on the ground are now presented on hardboard or canvas and painted with acrylic paints and brushes.

There are numerous other examples. The women at Ernabella in South Australia have adapted their ceremonial designs into a form of abstract patterning using colours such as red and blue. There are silk screen enterprises, such as at Bathurst Island where the Tiwi use their traditional designs on cloth to be marketed as wall-hangings, dress material, table cloths and scarves. There are pottery ventures. One potter, producing distinctive work, is Thancoupie, a woman from Weipa. She received formal training as a ceramic artist at East Sydney Technical College, now the National Art School. Having mastered her craft she began incorporating the stories of her people into designs to decorate the pots. She has since won Australia-wide recognition as a ceramicist.

Thancoupie, a distinguished ceramicist, making a *love magic* pot. ▶

Thancoupie – Garden pot.

Decorated emu egg.

Victorian Aboriginal artist, **Lynn Onus** and his work.

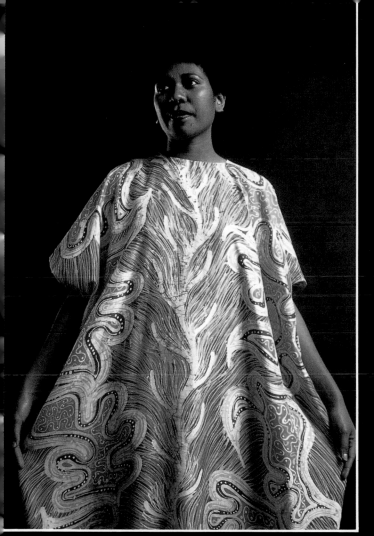

Tiwi fashions incorporating silk screen printing.

Silk screen printing, Bathurst Island, Northern Territory.

Ewald Namatjira – water colour painting in the representational manner.

Other artists produce work which is more European in style. The most obvious example is Albert Namatjira (1920-1959) who mastered the skills of water colour painting. He and his followers paint the landscape in a European representational manner, which doesn't aim to interpret the landscape. Artist Trevor Nickolls has had formal training as a painter in art schools in South Australia and Victoria. Recognition of his work came when he won a Creative Arts Fellowship to the Australian National University. Other artists have illustrated collections of traditional stories. Dick Roughsey (Goobalathaldin), a Lardil man from Mornington Island, has illustrated several picture books for children which have won him national and international acclaim. In recent years he has collaborated with Percy Trezise in producing further picture books based on the Quinkin spirits of the Laura area in Cape York.

Richard Barnes.

Jimmy Pike – Black and white work.

Percy Trezise and **Goobalathaldin (Dick) Roughsey** – Successful children's picture book collaborators, North Queensland. ▶

Trevor Nickolls – mural on a Melbourne tram.

Aboriginal contemporary art is very wide ranging. Not only is it produced in a traditional religious context but it is also being produced for the contemporary fine art scene, on both the national and international levels. The art presents a continuum extending from largely traditional motivations to those which are essentially European. The continuum reflects the diversity of Aboriginal life-styles that exist in this country. This introduction to Aboriginal art aims to heighten awareness of Aboriginal art, to develop an appreciation for it. It is an art founded in great antiquity which continues to be relevant in this modern world. As such it is a precious part of every Australian's heritage.

◀ **Painter of the future?** – Maningrida Pre-School, Arnhem Land, Northern Territory.

Bibliography

BERNDT, R.M., BERNDT, C.H., and STANTON, J.E. *Aboriginal Australian Art: a Visual Perspective,* Sydney, Methuen, 1982.

COOKE, P. 'Introduction' pp.5 in P. Cooke and J. Altman (eds.) *Aboriginal Art at the Top: a Regional Exhibition,* Maningrida, N.T., Maningrida Arts and Crafts, 1982.

COOPER, C. 'Art of temperate Southeast Australia' pp.29-41 in *Aboriginal Australia,* Sydney, Australian Gallery Directors Council, 1981.

GODDEN, E. *Rock Paintings of Aboriginal Australia,* French's Forest, N.S.W., Reed, 1982.

MORPHY, H. 'The art of northern Australia' pp.53-65 in *Aboriginal Australia,* Sydney, Australian Gallery Directors Council, 1981.

MULVANEY, J. 'Origins' pp.15-27 in *Aboriginal Australia,* Sydney, Australian Gallery Directors Council, 1981.

PETERSON, N. 'Art of the desert' pp.43-51 in *Aboriginal Australia,* Sydney, Australian Gallery Directors Council, 1981.

BOOKS FOR FURTHER READING

ABORIGINAL ARTS BOARD, *Oenpelli Bark Paintings,* Sydney, Ure Smith, 1979.

Aboriginal Australia, Sydney, Australian Gallery Directors Council, 1981.

BARDON, G. *Aboriginal Art of the Western Desert,* Adelaide, Rigby, 1979.

BERNDT, R.M., BERNDT, C.H., and STANTON, J.E. *Aboriginal Australian Art: a Visual Perspective,* Sydney, Methuen, 1982.

BRANDL, E.J. *Australian Aboriginal Paintings in Western and Central Arnhem Land ...,* Canberra, Australian Institute of Aboriginal Studies, 1973.

COOKE, P. and ALTMAN, J., eds. *Aboriginal Art at the Top: a Regional Exhibition,* Maningrida, N.T., Maningrida Arts and Crafts, 1982.

CRAWFORD, I.M. *The Art of the Wandjina: Aboriginal Cave Paintings in Kimberley, Western Australia,* Melbourne, Oxford University Press, 1968.

EDWARDS, R. *Australian Aboriginal Art: the Art of the Alligator Rivers Region, Northern Territory,* Canberra, Australian Institute of Aboriginal Studies, 1979.

GODDEN, E. *Rock Paintings of Aboriginal Australia,* photographed by J. Malnic, French's Forest, N.S.W., Reed, 1982.

ISAACS, J. *Thancoupie the Potter,* Sydney, The Aboriginal Artists Agency, 1982.

LOVEDAY, P. and COOKE, P., eds. *Aboriginal Arts and Crafts and the Market,* Darwin, The Australian National University North Australia Research Unit, 1983.

Mr Sandman Bring Me a Dream, Sydney, Papunya Tula Artists and the Aboriginal Artists Agency, 1981.

MUNN, N.D. *Walbiri Iconography: Graphic Representation and Cultural Symbolism in a Central Australian Society,* Ithaca, Cornell University Press, 1973.

TREZISE, P.J., *Rock Art of South-east Cape York,* Canberra, Australian Institute of Aboriginal Studies, 1971.

UCKO, P., ed. *Form in Indigenous Art: Schematisation in the Art of Aboriginal Australia and Prehistoric Europe,* Canberra, Australian Institute of Aboriginal Studies, 1978.

Torres Strait

Oenpelli
Maningrida
Melville Island
Ramingining
Bathurst Island
Yirrkala
Darwin
Kakadu
Cape York
Groote Eylandt
ARNHEM LAND
Laura
KIMBERLEYS

NORTHERN TERRITORY

Pilbara

Papunya
QUEENSLAND
Alice Springs

WESTERN AUSTRALIA

Ernabella
Brisbane

SOUTH AUSTRALIA

NEW SOUTH WALES

NULLABOR PLAIN
Koonalda
FLINDERS RANGES

Perth

Lake Mungo
Sydney
Adelaide
Kow Swamp
VICTORIA
Melbourne
Lake Tyers

TASMANIA
Hobart